HENLEY HERITAGE

Written and Illustrated by Jan Baldwin

First published by
Gresham Books
Henley-on-Thames
Oxfordshire, England

ISBN 0 946095 30 2

Desktop publishing by Elizabeth Wilsey
Printed and bound by Staples Printers, Kettering

HENLEY HERITAGE

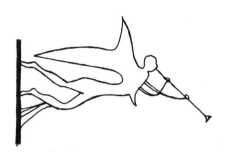

The illustrations in this book were chosen before I wrote about them. I selected them at random for their attractive appearance and because they were great fun to draw and paint. The accompanying essays taught me much more about Henley itself however, as each successive picture became more and more intricately interwoven into a whole and, I hope, coherent story.

I am grateful to all who helped me make this book possible.

*   *   *

"Henley-upon-Thames is a clean and cheerful town, in the hundred of Binfield and county of Oxford, situated near the base of a cluster of hills, in one of the most agreeable windings of the River Thames."

(*A Guide to Henley-on-Thames and its Vicinity,* printed and published by E. Kinch, Market Place 1866)

*   *   *   *   *

Henley Regatta in the Thirties – an Oarsman's Memory

"The sheer joy of the occasion was just the same: the sparkling water, the rose-clad wall of Phyllis Court opposite, brilliant green lawns, flowers everywhere; bright and chattering girls in pretty summer frocks and frilly hats; elderly oarsmen in pink socks; and Pimm's in profusion. Against this scene of gaiety, with punts crowded along the booms and the same umpires' launches following the races, was the glorious backdrop of the Chilterns, combining to lift the heart and for a while to be completely carefree.

Towards the end of the thirties we all knew that war was inevitable and imminent but somehow it cast no shadow over our happiness."

*   *   *   *   *

"Alice Springs is at the heart of the Red Centre of Australia, almost a thousand miles from the nearest capital city. The Todd River, which runs through the town, is dry except after flash floods, but this does not stop the locals holding their annual Henley-on-Todd Regatta in October. The boats are carried, or fitted with wheels, for the occasion."

(*Explore Australia: the Complete BP Touring Companion,* published by Viking O'Neill, 1994)

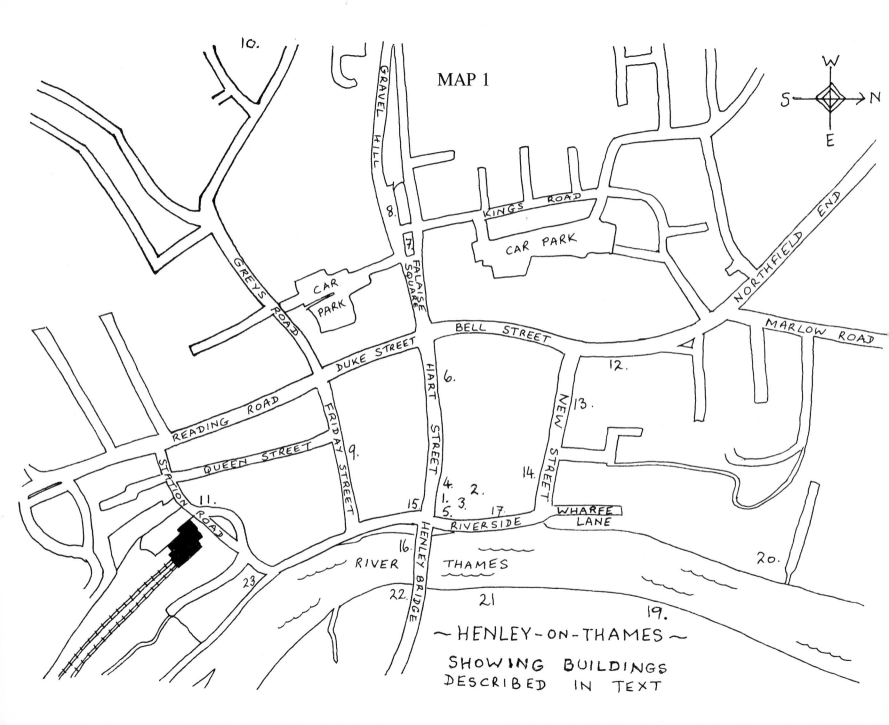

MAP 1

SHOWING BUILDINGS
DESCRIBED IN TEXT

~HENLEY-ON-THAMES~

CONTENTS

The Town

The River

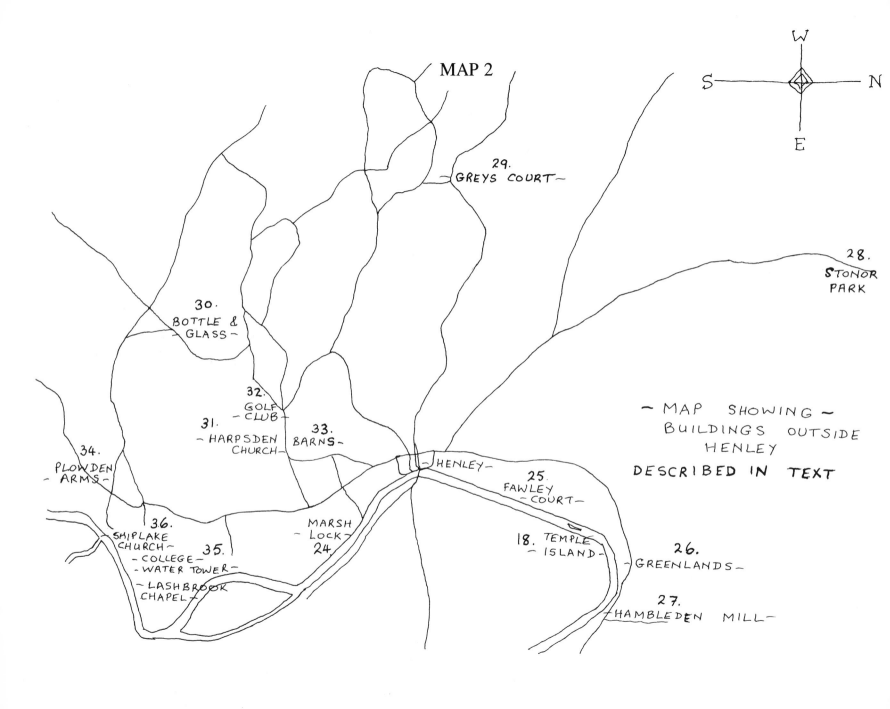

MAP 2

W
S — N
E

29.
GREYS COURT

28.
STONOR
PARK

30.
BOTTLE &
GLASS

32.
GOLF
CLUB

31.
HARPSDEN
CHURCH

33.
BARNS

34.
PLOWDEN
ARMS

HENLEY

25.
FAWLEY
COURT

~ MAP SHOWING ~
BUILDINGS OUTSIDE
HENLEY
DESCRIBED IN TEXT

36.
SHIPLAKE
CHURCH
COLLEGE
WATER TOWER
LASHBROOK
CHAPEL

35.

MARSH
LOCK
24.

18. TEMPLE
ISLAND

26.
GREENLANDS

27.
HAMBLEDEN MILL

CONTENTS

The Countryside

❧❧ HART STREET AND THE PARISH CHURCH ❧❧

HART Street is the best known of all roads in Henley. Coming over the bridge it is very impressive to pass through the narrow entrance by the Church and discover this spacious thoroughfare lined with elegant brick or plaster-fronted houses and buildings.

Hart Street has existed from the thirteenth century when Henley was a thriving market town and a centre for corn dealers. It used to be divided by another row of houses down the centre known as Middle Row, but these were cleared away in 1790 to make the approaches to the new bridge less cluttered.

Some of the buildings that we know today include Longlands, where a future Bishop of Lincoln was born, and three famous inns – the Red Lion, the Old White Hart and the Catherine Wheel. On the southern side is the Speaker's house, birthplace in 1591 of William Lenthall (who became the Speaker of the Long Parliament); Brakspears wine-store; the Old Rope Walk (originally used for making rope); Savills, a beautiful Queen Anne building; and Barclays Bank built in 1896.

The most significant building in Hart Street is, of course, the Parish Church of St. Mary the Virgin. Its origins date from at least 1204. Extensive alterations and additions have occurred over the years. In about 1540 the square, perpendicular tower was completed in flint and stone. This was probably built by John Longland, Bishop of Lincoln at that time. The tower is 118 feet high and dominates Henley from all directions.

In 1852 the north wall was replaced, the old galleries and box pews removed, new seats and floors installed, and stained glass put into the windows. A new roof was built and a new clock added.

The church interior is very beautiful, and extensions include the Lady Chapel, the St. Leonard's Chapel, the Jesus Chapel and the Baptistry. There is a marble monument to Lady Elizabeth Periam, who founded the Henley Blue-Coat School, and who died in 1621.

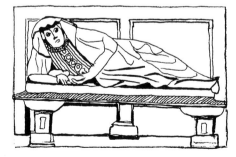

There is also a Rood Screen which commemorates those who fell in the two World Wars.

Perhaps the happiest memory one can have of Henley is to hear the church bells ringing on a summer's day, and to see the Cross of St. George flying from the Tower – preferably from a punt on the river!

MORNING COFFEE
LUNCHEONS
TEAS

LUNCHEONS
LICENSED

❧❧ THE ALMSHOUSES ❧❧

THERE are nineteen almshouses in St Mary's Churchyard, and they make a very attractive picture as one walks through the gardens past the Chantry House. The initial benefactor was John Longland, a Henley man born in 1473. His birthplace was the beautiful house nearby known as Longlands, which can be seen today, virtually unchanged.

John Longland became a fellow of Magdalen College, Oxford, and was ordained in 1500, later becoming Bishop of Lincoln and Confessor to Henry VIII. He was also Lord High Almoner and is remembered for two great endowments to Henley: the Church Tower and eight almshouses.

Originally these almshouses were on a site bought for ten pounds, south of the old wooden bridge and near where the Angel Inn is today. Five elderly men in one house, and three elderly women in another, each received fourpence a week towards their upkeep.

When the new bridge was erected in 1786 the almshouses were pulled down to make the approaches wider. They were rebuilt on land purchased by the Corporation with money from the bridge commissioners, next to the church and behind Longlands house. In 1830 these original eight houses plus an additional four made up the twelve charming terraced cottages which form the Longlands almshouses we can see today.

On the east side of the church yard are more almshouses which were endowed by Humphrey Newberry in 1664. At first there were ten one-storey almshouses, but by 1844 they were in such a state of disrepair it was necessary to rebuild them. Adjoining are four more almshouses given by Mrs Ann Messenger in 1669, and these also had to be replaced in 1846.

Longlands

Nowadays all these dwellings on the east side of St. Mary's churchyard have been enlarged by combining two cottages into one, so that there are seven homes instead of fourteen.

This hidden corner of Henley is a pleasant place to sit quietly for a while, and go back in time. The only intruders amongst the tombstones could well be a few friendly ducks, a reminder that the river is not far away.

Ian Baldwin '92

THE CHANTRY HOUSE

IN the Church garden on the north-eastern side of St. Mary's is the oldest house in Henley. It is a very fine half-timbered building known as the Chantry House. It is said to date from the fourteenth century when it was built to house the Chantry priests. These priests were endowed by wealthy people who paid large sums of money for them to sing masses for the salvation of their souls. Monks and abbots from Dorchester also lodged there.

Later, after passing through many hands, the Chantry House was eventually acquired by the Town Corporation. In 1602 the Grammar School was founded by King James I and initially housed there. In 1609 Lady Periam founded her school for twenty poor boys from Henley. The Grammar School was on the top floor and Lady Periam's School was on the floor below. In 1846 the Red Lion Hotel bought the Chantry House which became part of the inn until 1920.

At the end of the first World War the Chantry House was purchased, restored and presented to the Parish Church in memory of the Reverend Canon John Frederic Maul who had been a rector there for many years and had died in 1915. It is now connected by a passageway to the Church and is used as a centre for the social life of the parish.

There are three storeys to the Chantry House, but from the Church garden only the upper two can be seen. The lowest floor is part of the courtyard of the Red Lion Hotel and is visible only from that side. The interior of the uppermost floor is lined with ancient timberwork still in a good state of preservation.

Because of its secluded position tucked away amongst the almshouses it is easy to miss seeing altogether, but it is well worth seeking out, due to its historical interest and tranquil setting.

Jan Baldwin 1989

❧❧❧ TWO MONUMENTS ❧❧❧

THE ornate, Victorian drinking-fountain in this picture was erected in the Market Place in 1885 by the family and friends of the late Rev. Greville Phillimore in memory of his services as Rector of Henley. It was known as the Phillimore Memorial Fountain and replaced the Obelisk which had previously been there. The fountain steps became a favourite place for those who sold lavender, and for a time was surrounded by four lamps.

In 1903, as the amount of traffic increased, the fountain was moved from the centre of Henley to a position on the southern side of Bishop Longland's almshouses near the west entrance door of St. Mary's Church. It has ceased to have water supplied for many years but remains part of Henley's history.

*   *   *   *   *

The Obelisk

The Obelisk which was at the crossroads before being replaced by the fountain, originally had a pump attached for washing the narrow streets, particularly after market days. Before the present bridge was built, there was an extra row of houses down the middle of Hart Street and Market Place. When they were demolished in 1790 to make the approaches to the new bridge more accessible, street-washing became less necessary and the obelisk had its pump removed. It then acted as a signpost to London and Reading.

After the Phillimore fountain was built, the obelisk was moved to Northfield End in 1886, at the junction with Marlow Road. It remained there until 1970 when a new road system was introduced. It now stands proudly in Mill Meadows serving as a link with the past.

Both these monuments concern the use of water in the town, one for cleaning the streets and the other for drinking. Today they are reminders of Henley's heritage.

THE RED LION HOTEL

THIS famous old coaching-inn by the bridge probably had its origins in 1531, possibly to accommodate the craftsmen and their apprentices who were constructing the tower of St. Mary's Church nearby.

Its situation overlooking the river has always been a great attraction to visitors, many of whom have been famous. Charles I stayed here en route from London to Oxford in 1632 and again ten years later with Prince Rupert. In 1889 his coat of arms was discovered, painted above a fireplace in one of the upstairs bedrooms. This is now carefully preserved. The Duke of Marlborough had his own room which he used when travelling to Blenheim. Other celebrated visitors include the poet Shenstone, Dr. Johnson and James Boswell, George III with his wife and daughters, and George IV when he was Prince Regent. A more recent royal visitor was the late Princess Grace in 1947 when her brother was competing in the Regatta. For many years bedrooms in the hotel were named after their illustrious guests.

The Red Lion has always been closely associated with the bridge, whose design plans of 1781 can be seen today in the Hotel. Being so much a part of the river, the inn hosted the first Oxford and Cambridge University Boat Race crews in 1829. Ten years after this successful occasion the first Henley Regatta took place, with races ending at the bridge. Hotel residents could have a marvellous view from the lawns which swept down to the water's edge, until the present road cut their access.

In 1846 the Red Lion bought the Chantry House which was used for hotel purposes until the parish acquired it again in 1920. In June 1857 the branch railway-line from Twyford to Henley was opened. This marked the end of the era of the four-horse coaches which had run twice daily from the Hotel to Twyford and back, to connect with the main London line.

In 1897 the Red Lion was described as "no longer an old-world coaching-inn, but a fashionable hotel," complete with fine new entrance porch, and plenty of palms and ferns inside.

Nowadays the boathouses next to the stables have become the Century Galleries. The hotel itself is still a Henley landmark where travellers can be assured of "the warmest welcome."

Century Galleries

THE RED LION HOTEL

RED
LION
HOTEL

Ian Baldwin '89

❧❧❧ THE CATHERINE WHEEL ❧❧❧

T HE Catherine Wheel is a large and very old hotel in Hart Street. Dating back to 1541, it is named after St. Catherine, a former favourite saint of Henley. In St. Mary's Church there was a chapel dedicated to her.

St. Catherine of Alexandria is reputed to have courted martyrdom by making open confession of the gospel in defiance of the Emperor Maximin. She was tortured, and then placed on a toothed wheel which is said to have fallen to pieces at her touch. It is the origin of the Catherine Wheel in fireworks displays. In the Middle Ages she was the patron saint of wheelwrights.

For a few years during the seventeenth century the Catherine Wheel issued token money used by Henley tradesmen to supplement the national currency. Bronze or copper tokens were given as change and could be redeemed later with real money. By the end of the eighteenth century it was one of four main coaching inns in the town. With twenty-four coaches passing through daily, Henley was a staging post for London, Oxford and many other places further afield.

Being so centrally situated the Catherine Wheel has featured in many local events. At the end of the nineteenth century hunting meets were known to have assembled there. The hotel was then in its heyday, providing all types of refreshments, good accommodation and "an omnibus and carriages to meet all trains." Above all, there was an excellent billiard-room!

There was a good working relationship with Brakspear's brewery until the Catherine Wheel became a member of the Berni Inn group more recently. No longer providing bedrooms, it has instead a reputation for being an ideal place for families to enjoy a meal out together. The saint may no longer be remembered on the feast-day of St. Catherine's on the 25th November, but she can still be seen with her wheel on the inn-sign outside.

*   *   *

Nearby, the Old White Hart, after which Hart Street is named, is even more ancient. The inner courtyard behind used to have a gallery all round it, from where bull-baiting and cock-fighting could be watched.

THE TOWN HALL

THE Town Hall is the focal point of Henley's administration. Its situation in Falaise Square, formerly called the Market Place, is a central and commanding one.

On this site there used to be a Guildhall, which fell into disrepair in about 1760. As the old wooden bridge also collapsed in a flood in 1774 after twenty years of disuse, the residents of Henley were without both a Guildhall and a bridge for quite a long time.

The decision to go ahead with a new and larger Town Hall in the centre of the Market Place was made during this period. In 1795 the replacement was completed by William Bradshaw, a member of the Corporation. It was a handsome, colonnaded building which must have made a very favourable impression to all who entered the town, especially by way of the new bridge and along Hart Street.

However it was a relatively short-lived structure. Although it was added to in 1870 by enclosing some of the ground floor area used as a corn market, it was decided to build a larger and newer Town Hall to commemorate Queen Victoria's Diamond Jubilee. This was completed in 1901.

The old Town Hall was not entirely forgotten, however. It was carefully dismantled and rebuilt in Crazies Hill as a private house where it still stands today.

Henley's Town Hall contains many fine paintings including some by John Piper and has a large main hall which can be used for meetings and functions as well as being the headquarters for the Town Council. Henley was granted a coat of arms in 1974 when it ceased to be a borough and the Town Council became the governing body, with a Town Mayor and sixteen councillors.

Market Place became known as Falaise Square in the same year following Henley's twinning with Falaise in Normandy. The pollarded trees and small square add an interesting Gallic touch to this very English Thameside town.

The Old Town Hall

🌿🌿 THE MARKET PLACE 🌿🌿

THE market place in Henley today is a small area behind the Town Hall. Originally it covered a large part of the town centre, including what is now called Falaise Square.

From the middle ages Henley was a commercial and trading centre. Because of its situation by the river, there was boat-building, and the town was also a base for the transportation of goods such as timber, wool, corn and malt. As the roads improved, more wagon traffic passed through as well, from London, Oxford, Reading and numerous other places. All this activity was good for business and many inns flourished as a result.

The weekly market was held on Thursdays. It not only filled the centre round the old Guildhall from Gravel Hill down to Hart Street, but also included the whole of Friday Street and New Street. From early morning stalls were crammed into all available spaces, selling vegetables of many kinds, and eggs, fish, meat, lace and glassware. Animals were penned nearby and agricultural implements were on sale. Wagons filled with corn and carts full of goods were all part of the noisy, bustling scene.

Market Place was also the site of many fairs, usually held about three times a year, but these ended in 1876. The market place's domination of the town declined with the coming of the railways, when Henley was initially by-passed and lost a certain amount of trade.

In 1974 the large part of the market place in front of the Town Hall was renamed Falaise Square. In today's considerably reduced market place behind the Town Hall are some interesting Georgian buildings. Stuart Turner Ltd. now occupies the premises which previously formed the sixteenth-century Broad Gates Inn. Other buildings include the Baptist Church, the Malt House, the fire station, an Exhibition Centre, the Victoria Inn, and various shops and restaurants as well as private houses. Gravel Hill leads up to Friar Park and Badgemore Country Club, and still has a raised, cobbled pavement. The few market-stalls set up below every Thursday are a reminder of another era when Henley made its living as a market-town.

Jan Baldwin '91

❧❧ FRIDAY STREET ❧❧

FRIDAY Street used to form the southern boundary of Henley, and overlooked open countryside which was in the parish of Rotherfield Greys. It was a poor road, and its inhabitants were hard-working and tough.

These conditions are hard to visualise today, as most of the small industries carried out in the street over the years have now disappeared. Almost all of the original buildings have been restored to a high standard. However, a glance at some of the names of the houses brings back memories of the past.

A grain store existed on the north corner facing the river. This beautifully converted old building is now known as "The Old Granary" and very much enhances that part of Henley's waterfront, together with Barn Cottage, Friday Cottage and Old Timbers in Friday Street itself. The Doll's House, pink-fronted and bent with age, comes next in the row. Inside, it has a "thieves' step" with an extra large tread at the bottom to trip up any unwary burglar making a quick exit!

Opposite, Baltic Cottage is a reminder of the Henley base of the Baltic Mercantile and Shipping Exchange. Grey's Brewery has gone, also a tannery and a foundry. However, Queen Anne Cottage is now the name of the restored property on the site of the tannery.

Two inns which are no longer there are the White Lion Hotel, and the Black Horse Inn, both now private houses. There is, however, still the Anchor Inn with the familiar Brakspear's sign on it, standing next to the former Grey's Brewery site.

Although the old printing works and paper bag factory have disappeared, plenty of other small businesses and shops abound, ranging from antiques and books to motor accessories, and from Chinese takeaways to opticians. Today's Friday Street is very much part of modern everyday life, while still retaining a charming and nostalgic picture of an earlier period.

The Anchor Inn

Ian Baldwin '89

ROTHERFIELD COURT

ROTHERFIELD Court stands on the high land above Henley known as Ancastle. In 1860 the Rev. Dr. Morrell, who was Rector at the time, bought the property and built the house, which was sold to Colonel Makins twelve years later. The Colonel enlarged both the house and grounds and is remembered for having a stained glass window put in the South Chapel of St. Mary's Church in 1885 in memory of two earlier bishops from Henley.

The house itself, however, was destined to become the centre of education in Henley. This began in 1604 when King James I granted a Charter for a Grammar School, with an annual endowment of £11.17s.4d.

In 1609 Lady Elizabeth Periam founded and endowed a charity school for twenty poor boys to be taught writing, reading and craft apprenticeship. These two schools were initially set up in the Chantry House, the upper floor being used for the Grammar School and the lower floor by Lady Periam's school.

In 1778 the two schools were joined by an act of Parliament into the United Charity Schools of Henley-on-Thames. The funds were combined and one body of trustees managed them both. But they still remained quite distinct, the "Upper School" being the Henley Royal Grammar School, and the "Lower School" continuing as before.

As numbers increased the whole school moved from the Chantry house to what had formerly been the Bell Inn, in 1841. However, due to lack of space, the Lower School went to old premises behind the Speaker's house in Hart Street.

By 1928 the school had grown so much it moved to the house that Colonel Makins had improved and enlarged in Victorian times: Rotherfield Court. This fine old residence was altered yet again to accommodate four hundred boys and girls, and became a co-educational County Council School. By 1974 it was known as King James's College of Henley and was the first sixth-form college in the county.

The merging of this school with the South Oxfordshire Technical College in 1987 resulted in "The Henley College", which was the first tertiary college in Oxfordshire. Rotherfield Court, built as a private house, is now an excellent centre for Henley's large educational establishment.

Jan Baldwin '93

❧❧❧ THE IMPERIAL HOTEL ❧❧❧

THE Imperial Hotel is a delightfully flamboyant example of its period. Built in the early part of this century at the height of the British Empire, its name is certainly appropriate. For a brief time recently it was known as the Edwardian Hotel, but it reverted to its original name in March 1993 when its new owner gave it a face-lift.

Due to the increasing popularity of the Henley Regatta last century, more and more visitors were flocking to the town every summer for this event. As day-trips from London and elsewhere were made possible with the opening of the branch line of the railway from Twyford to Henley, the Regatta's success was assured. It also meant that more hotels could make a good business accommodating guests as well.

When it was first built, the hotel's situation opposite the railway station was ideal for this custom. The attention to detail in the hotel's decoration is typical of its day, and this is reflected in the adjoining buildings with pleasing results. Known sometimes as Imperial Parade, the crescent must have made a welcoming sight to travellers on their arrival at Henley. The extra trains provided for the Regatta week were filled with passengers in splendid boating regalia – the ladies with sunhats, frills and parasols, the gentlemen in striped blazers and boaters. This scene is virtually unchanged today! The old station has gone, but the new one nearby, although less decorative, still copes with a huge influx of visitors whose regatta dress has changed little over the years.

Since its recent change-over and reversion to the name "Imperial", the hotel has acquired a far Eastern touch, due to the new owner's connections with Thailand. Interior decorations of ornate wooden banisters from Edwardian days blend successfully with the oriental carvings now incorporated on the landings and in the bedrooms. In the Bangkok Bar, a nineteenth century photograph of

The Old Railway Station

Rama V, King of Siam, makes a handsome centrepiece, and the pictures in the halls depict scenes from that country's history. Steps lead up to the dining-room, whose focal point is a model of an intricate Thai Temple, lit by candles at night. Staff from Thailand wearing national dress provide an oriental atmosphere which adds an exotic touch to the Thames Valley.

RUPERT HOUSE SCHOOL

RUPERT House is another educational establishment in Henley which has an interesting historical background. The building itself, adjacent to the house called Countess Gardens, is of Georgian origin. Its site, which was part of a large area from New Street to Bell Lane, and from Bell Street to Wharfe Lane, was also known as Countess Gardens and contained a manor house from the early fourteenth century.

During the civil war Henley was forced into supporting the Roundhead faction, as its most prominent citizen, Sir Bulstrode Whitelock of Fawley Court was, due to his legal interests, a Parliamentarian. When the Roundheads, based at Phyllis Court, clashed with the Royalists garrisoned at Fawley Court and later at Greenlands, Henley itself became drawn into the conflict.

The dashing young Prince Rupert, a cousin of King Charles I, was in charge of these Royalist troops while they were in Henley. In 1643 the Roundheads marched to Henley from Windsor to find that the Royalists had damaged the bridge and fled. They later returned under Prince Rupert from Reading, but were defeated in the "Battle of Duke Street". Prince Rupert, however, seems to have been chiefly remembered for hanging a Parliamentary spy in 1642 on a large elm tree outside the Bell Inn. Needless to say the tree itself suffered a sticky end when it succumbed to Dutch Elm disease in the 1970s.

Rupert House School is one of many buildings in this area which have named themselves after the Prince. In 1934, when it was 90 Bell Street, the property was sold to Miss Hallett and Miss Verrall as a day and boarding school called St. Joan's. This had previously been a dance school next to the Kenton theatre. In 1946 the school was called Rupert House, and in 1956 it became a non profit-making company. Today it is registered as a charity and is a member of the Independent Association of Preparatory Schools. It caters for day girls up to the age of thirteen and also has a few very young boys. The pupils work in a house set in a corner of Henley amongst medieval buildings, from private malt houses to granaries, reminders of the brewing industry that still flourishes.

*   *   *

Nearby, Rupert Cottage is a charming private residence dating from 1530, when it was called Apple Warren Farmhouse. King Zog of Albania, exiled to Britain in World War Two, is reputed to have stayed there.

NEW STREET AND THE KENTON THEATRE

WHEN New Street came into existence over six hundred years ago, it formed the northern limit of the town of Henley. Over the years it became the centre of the Corn Market and in 1658 was the site of the first Quaker meeting. Ambrose Rigg would stable his horse at the Rose and Crown Inn, and preach his doctrine to those attending the market in the road.

There are several buildings in New Street which have remained unspoilt to this day. Early fifteenth century houses, Georgian and Victorian properties blend together to make a pleasant picture. Until 1967 the pavements on each side of the road were still bordered with a shallow gully of rounded cobbles for the horse traffic of many years before.

The Kenton Theatre, originally known as the New Theatre, was built on land owned by Robert Kenton more than a hundred and fifty years earlier. He left the site to the Henley Corporation, and the five houses on it at the time were used as the town's workhouse until 1790. In 1805 it was leased to Sampson Penley and John Jonas who were experienced and well-travelled actors, determined to build a permanent theatre.

In November 1805, the first performance held was the comedy *The School of Reform,* or *How to Rule a Husband.* Tickets varied from four shillings for boxes to one shilling in the gallery. In December there was a charity performance of *The Rivals* by Sheridan, for the benefit of widows and orphans of the brave men who fell in the "glorious victories" at Trafalgar.

However business became slack and in 1813 the lease was sold. The theatre was used for a variety of other purposes. It was only in the 1930s that it was used again for plays, and in 1951 a new proscenium and arch was designed and painted by John Piper. In 1965 it was saved from demolition by local residents who set about a complete restoration.

Today, this attractive theatre is the fourth oldest in England to survive and remain in use, after those in Bristol, Margate and Richmond in Yorkshire. It is kept in use by local drama and opera groups and societies with occasional performances by visiting professionals.

Ian Baldwin

❧❧ HENLEY BREWERY ❧❧

"Good ale, the true and proper drink of Englishmen"

AS George Borrow said, beer was indeed the staple drink of the English. This was largely due to the dubious quality of the drinking water. Because of its bulk it was produced for local markets, so throughout the country the towns had brewers who were skilled at this work. Henley was well-known for its brewing industry, being a market-centre for corn, and famous also for its malting skills. It also had a plentiful supply of well-water, all combining to make it an ideal base for brewing.

In 1779 Robert Brakspear, the son of a Faringdon tailor, came to Henley to work at his uncle's brewery in Bell Street. When his uncle retired sixteen years later, he owned and was managing the business single-handed. He kept well abreast of all the latest technology, coping with his rivals and persuading publicans to distribute his particular brand. In 1812 he had founded a dynasty which continued with his second son, William, then only ten years old.

Fourteen years later William Brakspear became a partner, greatly expanding the firm by buying up property, especially public-houses. By 1847 the brewery was supplying eighty-seven tied houses. When he died aged eighty, he had been a justice of the peace, an alderman and four times mayor. He was mourned by Henley as one of the town's "oldest and most respected townsmen." In the evening a muffled peal was rung on the bells of the parish church.

He was succeeded by two of his sons, Archibald and George. With the purchase of Grey's Brewery in 1896 there were 150 public-houses owned by the firm which now became a limited company, moving to the present site in New Street, virtually unchanged today. The brewery is on the south side, and opposite is the malthouse. In 1909 Archibald Rowsell Brakspear succeeded as Chairman, acquiring the Wokingham Brewery, while his son later bought Grundy's Brewery in Goring. The sixth generation member, Paul Brakspear, is now Trade Director and Michael Chalcraft is Chairman. Of all the old breweries in Henley, Brakspear's is the sole survivor, supplying 130 picturesque public-houses in the beautiful countryside of South Oxfordshire.

Tradition has it that as long as the holly and mistletoe branches placed on a beam in the brewery courtyard every Christmas hang securely, the firm will continue to prosper.

Ian Baldwin '92

THE ANGEL ON THE BRIDGE

THIS is undoubtedly the best known view of Henley. Apart from its attractive appearance, it incorporates many features of the town together, each representing a different aspect of its history.

St. Mary's Church, particularly its tower, dominates the scene. The Red Lion Hotel on the right is famous both for its great age and for the celebrities who have stayed there. The lovely stone bridge blends into the picture, providing a perfect setting for the Angel Hotel. The riverside houses and towpath which continue to the left have all played a part in Henley's development.

The Angel on the Bridge, as we call the hotel today, was built in the eighteenth century. Full of quaint rooms and passageways, with bay windows overlooking the bridge and river, its direct waterfront terrace makes it unique in Henley. By the end of the nineteenth century it had become a favourite spot for fishermen and artists alike. The advent of the Regatta also made it a popular base from which to hire pleasure boats.

To the left of the picture stands the former Rectory, part of which dates from 1700. This is now owned by the investment company, Perpetual. Along the riverside are more charming old buildings with weathered red-tiled rooftops, all of which have been converted into houses or shops, yet still outwardly retaining the character of a bygone era.

On the river in summer there is a pageant of constantly changing scenes as the boats pass by: punts, canoes, skiffs, launches and other motor vessels. Not only boats – there are ducks, coots, moorhens, grebes, Canada geese and swans. The swans are identified and marked and most are

owned by the Queen. The geese arrived a few years ago on their way south and seem to have settled here in large numbers. All are looked after well both by residents and visitors. It has been known for a policeman to stop the traffic to allow a mother duck with her babies to cross the road safely!

Perpetual Investment Management Services Ltd

HENLEY BRIDGE

ISIS

TAMESIS

HENLEY'S lovely stone bridge has been a striking feature of the town since it was built in the eighteenth century. On each of its corners are famous buildings: the Angel on the Bridge, the Red Lion Hotel, the Leander Club and the Regatta Headquarters.

The importance of having a bridge had always been realised from ancient Roman times. In the Middle Ages a wooden structure on stone foundations was built, on which there were actually a few houses, an inn and a chapel. There was also a close connection between St. Mary's Church and the bridge.

During the Civil War it became badly damaged and as time went by more and more repairs were needed to keep it in use. By 1754 it was declared too dangerous, and a ferry boat was provided by the Town Corporation as an alternative means of crossing the river. Twenty years later a terrible flood swept the whole bridge away, but it was another seven years before an act of Parliament authorised the building of a replacement.

The architect for the new bridge was William Hayward of Shrewsbury, and stone from Headington Quarry was used. By 1786 it was completed at a cost of £10,000. A toll was charged for this, and continued for eighty-seven years when, no doubt to the relief of Henley residents, it was finally paid off.

The five arches of the bridge are particularly attractive in their design. On the keystones of the central one, Mrs. Anne Danner carved two faces: Tamesis, the male head, looking downstream, and Isis, the female head, looking upstream. They are said to represent the fabled marriage between the Thame and the Isis when they unite into one river at Dorchester.

The general effect of the bridge is very pleasing to the eye, with its gracious curve and balustrades along each side. Long may it withstand any future heavy flooding, as well as coping with an ever-increasing volume of heavy road traffic!

Jan Baldwin 1993

❧❧ RIVERSIDE SCENE ❧❧

THIS most attractive view of Henley's riverside shows a variety of buildings which together tell a significant story. The river itself is part of the history too, for this was as far upstream as most of the barge traffic reached in medieval times. The arches of the old wooden bridge would have restricted further navigation by large barges.

Heavy goods were unloaded here and transported by road to Wallingford and Oxford. In turn, corn and timber were brought down from the Chilterns to be sent by river to London. The river trade and thriving boat-building industry were responsible for the early commercial success of Henley.

The town's cheese market used to be held at the end of New Street. The malting industry which flourished in those days gave Henley the reputation of trading mainly in "beer and boats". The breweries and boathouses set up were a symbol of the town's prosperity for many years to come.

With the advent of the railways Henley's trading future seemed threatened, not being on the main line to the west. The holding of a regatta in an attempt to attract visitors seemed a good idea, and the first one was at the end of the university year in 1839, ten years after the first Oxford and Cambridge boat race had been held from Hambleden to Henley. Initially the finish was at the bridge, and stands were erected outside the Red Lion Hotel, continuing down as far as New Street. As this function became more and more popular, the railway branch line was built which promoted yet more visitors. Later the Regatta enclosures were moved opposite and slightly downstream to Poplar Point, where the races could finish without negotiating a bend.

The buildings in the picture include Brakspear's brewery in the background, and the public slipway in front of New Street. Hobbs and Sons' boat business occupied the boathouses on the right, but these are now private dwellings. The painted narrow boat in the foreground is one of today's many pleasure boats seen on the Thames, which links up with all the canals and inland waterways of Britain.

❧❧❧ TEMPLE ISLAND ❧❧❧

DURING the eighteenth century the two most fashionable houses near Henley were Park Place and Fawley Court. Friendly rivalry existed between their owners during this period, each improving their already beautiful properties with lavish embellishments.

In 1771 Sambrooke Freeman and his wife, of Fawley Court, commissioned James Wyatt, a young twenty-five year old designer, to create an elegant folly, or summer-house, on their river island. The result was the delightful small temple which has since achieved fame as the starting-point of the Regatta Course.

When the first Regatta was held many years later, in the summer of 1839, four races were rowed from the top of Temple Island to Henley Bridge. This meant that the bend at Poplar Point, just before the winning-post, was unfair to the team on the outside. So in 1886 a "new course" was introduced which started at the bottom of Temple Island finishing at Poplar Point instead. But the prevailing south west wind sheltered the Buckinghamshire station crew more than the other. To counteract this the "straight course", used today, was first rowed in 1924, and required part of Temple Island and the Berkshire bank opposite to be dug away.

Temple Island was used by the Leander Club at the end of the last century as an enclosure during the building of its new clubhouse in Henley. Meanwhile the island's ownership passed from the Freemans to the MacKenzies of Fawley Court, and was acquired by Henley Regatta in 1987. Since then the somewhat dilapidated temple has been beautifully restored. This has involved conservation specialists removing several layers of paint to reveal the Etruscan-style decoration of the period, with delicate eighteenth century colours. A French marble statue of a Bacchante adorns the pillared dome, adding a charming touch to the completed work.

Each race is followed by one of the traditional umpire's launches, all of which have lovely names such as Enchantress, Amaryllis and Arethusa.

Ian Baldwin '89

HENLEY ROYAL REGATTA

IT is difficult to imagine Henley without a regatta. Every year at the end of June it is suddenly overwhelmed by thousands of visitors. Whether they come for the rowing itself or merely to revel in the atmosphere, this small Thameside town is transformed into the centre for a major event in the English season.

It all started in 1829 when Oxford and Cambridge held their boat-race from Hambleden to Henley. Large crowds came, boosting local trade, and it was obvious for the first time just how magnificent the straight stretch of river was from Temple Island to the bridge. In June 1839 the first Regatta was held, following a meeting attended by wealthy local citizens, at which the first stewards were selected. There were only two races that day, and the course length was one mile and 550 yards, ending by the bridge itself.

Henley Regatta received a Royal Patronage in 1851 from Prince Albert which successive monarchs have supported. It also prospered when the local railway branch line from Twyford opened, improving accessibility to visitors. The Golden Era of the Henley Royal Regatta was from 1870 to the outbreak of the First World War. Hundreds of punts and skiffs were out on the river, houseboats lined the banks and everyone enjoyed themselves hugely. Later, piles and booms marked out the course to prevent spectators' boats impeding the actual races. The Stewards Enclosure was opened in 1919 for smoother running of the Regatta with advance sales of entry tickets. It now includes members' stands, champagne and Pimm's bars, a bandstand, souvenir shop, lunch and tea tents. The trophies are all on display, including the Grand Challenge Cup, which dates back to the first Regatta.

Foreign crews started appearing in 1872 with the Americans who now have an impressive number of wins to their credit. Today crews come from all over the world to participate on this testing course, which has twice staged the rowing Olympics in 1908 and 1948.

Henley Royal Regatta is organised down to the last detail. Even the swans have to be removed from the river in preparation for the five-day event. The majority of pleasure boats are motor launches and steamers, but there are still traditional punts and skiffs providing a nostalgic atmosphere. The strict rules laid out for dress in the enclosure give a timeless feeling to the occasion. Apart from the high standard of rowing, Henley has been described as "the greatest water-picnic in the world".

Jan Baldwin
1991

PHYLLIS COURT

THE lovely mansion known as Phyllis Court is set in landscaped grounds by the river just north of Henley, on the site of the ancient moated manor originally called Fillets Court.

During the Civil War Phyllis Court was owned by Sir Bulstrode Whitelocke, Henley's most prominent citizen, whose main residence had been Fawley Court. Because of his parliamentary interests, Henley was committed to the Roundhead faction. The King had set up his headquarters in Oxford in 1642, and so for his protection Henley was occupied by Royalist forces under his nephew Prince Rupert. They were garrisoned at Fawley Court and Greenlands. When the parliamentarians re-occupied Henley in 1643, Phyllis Court was fortified by the Roundheads to counter these Royalist troops. Part of the riverside wall built by Oliver Cromwell can still be seen today. After the King escaped from Oxford and returned to London to surrender, Sir Bulstrode was allowed to dismantle the fort.

The house was altered by the various families who occupied it over the following years. Towards the end of the eighteenth century Phyllis Court was the centre of Henley's social scene along with Fawley Court and Park Place. In 1837 the house was demolished and rebuilt as we know it today. In 1900 it was unoccupied, becoming a club founded by Captain Roy Finlay in 1906.

From then on it prospered as a unique social club, catering especially for seasonal occasions such as Ascot and, in particular, Henley Regatta. In 1924 the Prince of Wales became its patron, and the mansion was by now considerably updated, with croquet lawns and tennis courts in the grounds. It was requisitioned for war use during the forties, reopening in 1946 when more refurbishment took place and two blocks of flats were built along the drive. The latest improvement has been the Grandstand Pavilion rebuilt in 1993 on the river bank, and winning a British Construction Industry Award.

Nowadays members can enjoy a full diary of social activities including bridge, discussion groups, musical evenings, dances, theatre outings and golf. But it is the five days of Henley Regatta that remains the ultimate period in Phyllis Court's calendar. This continues unchanged over the years, with deck-chairs on the lawn, the awning by the riverbank, and the military band playing, making it an ideal place to entertain visitors.

Jan Baldwin 1991

THE LEANDER CLUB

THE Leander Club is the oldest and most prestigious rowing club in the country. Its origins go back to 1818 when a group of fifteen men met regularly in various London boatyards to row together. The word Leander came from the name of a six-oared cutter, a popular racing boat of the period. In Greek mythology Leander was a youth who swam every night across the Hellespont to visit Hero, a priestess of Aphrodite. When he was drowned in a storm, Hero threw herself into the sea. The fortunes of the Leander Club have turned out much more happily.

By 1831 it had its own clubroom in a Lambeth boatyard, and at the first Henley Regatta in 1839 assisted in drawing up the rules, and provided the umpire. Leander won its first Grand Challenge Cup the following year. But the small membership numbers restricted any further success for some time. In 1858 some Oxford and Cambridge oarsmen, unable to form complete crews, were granted permission to combine and row under the distinct salmon pink blades. Thus began the strong connection between Leander and the two universities, and resulting increase in the Club size. By 1860 all restrictions on membership were removed. In 1866 Leander had its first permanent boathouse in Putney, next to the London Rowing Club. The rules for entry to the club for Oxbridge undergraduate oarsmen were made much more difficult in 1890, thereby making membership more attractive and competitive. This resulted in a higher standard and significant achievements; Leander won the Grand Challenge Trophy twelve times during the next fifteen years.

The Club moved to Henley during this period, firstly renting rooms at the old Royal Hotel, and creating an enclosure on Temple Island. By 1896 the present clubhouse was completed near the site of the old toll house by the bridge. Today it is very much part of the Regatta scene, in its premier position, with its gabled rooftops, glassed-in balconies and marquee on the lawn. The towpath in front is filled with throngs of visitors flocking to the races as they make their way past the striped boat-tents.

Leander's successes have continued both at the Regatta and the Olympics over the years, as well as at other international events. All clubmen are proud to wear the eye-catching pink tie and socks. With a membership of such distinguished rowing men who have devoted their lives to the sport it is indeed a unique establishment whose emblem is, curiously, a hippopotamus.

Ian Baldwin 1991

22

REGATTA HEADQUARTERS

FOR many years Henley Regatta was run without permanent headquarters. From 1901 to 1905 the stewards rented Phyllis Court during Regatta week only, leasing various other places over the years for their staff. When the opportunity came to buy the land occupied by the old Carpenters Arms and several neglected boat-sheds by the bridge, Terry Farrell was the architect chosen to design the new building. He must have found this a great challenge, and its situation at the very entrance to Henley an exciting one.

Described locally as a "Temple to the Sport of Rowing" the completed headquarters was officially opened by Her Majesty the Queen in 1986. Winner of several British design awards this contemporary building is spacious and light inside, offering lovely views of the Thames. From the overhanging balcony one can look across to the Angel on the Bridge and the row of Georgian houses to the left along the riverside.

The new building is on three floors, a wet boathouse for storage of Regatta equipment and an umpire's launch, with the level above used by office staff who were previously housed in two rooms of the Leander Club. There is a large reception area, a committee boardroom, a shop containing items sold at the Regatta, and lastly the trophies. These include the Ladies' Challenge Plate, the Thames Challenge Cup, the Princess Elizabeth Challenge Cup and the Visitors' Challenge Cup. The most prestigious of all is the Grand Challenge Cup, a magnificent trophy dating back to the very first Regatta held in 1839. On the top floor is an apartment for the Regatta Secretary.

Inside a dedicated staff work all the year round to ensure the Regatta runs smoothly. Membership badges are sent out, with dates and literature concerning the forthcoming season. Accommodation for the competitors is arranged using a scheme known as "the Regatta 'landladies'". These are local families prepared to host visiting crews for up to two or three weeks and make their stay in Henley more enjoyable. The course is marked out with piles and booms in April, and tents go up soon after.

Henley Royal Regatta Headquarters blends elegantly with the Georgian bridge and in time should give the impression of having been there forever – as with the Temple downstream where the races start.

Ian Baldwin

23

❧❧❧ HOBBS BOATHOUSE ❧❧❧

THE development of the pleasure boat industry came during the nineteenth century and gained momentum as the great old barges lost their trade. This was largely due to the coming of the railways which very much altered the transportation of bulky items previously dependent upon the river.

There had always been boatyards along Henley's riverside, and the large barges were moored up to deliver their goods north of the bridge itself. When the Regatta started in 1839 its success encouraged the building of smaller boats for people to buy or hire and use for enjoyment of the river.

In 1870 Hobbs and Sons Ltd was established at the end of New Street by the public slipway, in two old boat-houses. They became well-known for their river-craft of all descriptions, and were able to accommodate two hundred boats. They advertised two steam launches available for trips, the *Marian* and the *Ghoorkha,* and they built all sorts of pleasure boats from punts to canoes. They also offered hiring and storage facilities.

The premises are now at the corner of Station Road and the river, and true to tradition, boats are hired, repaired, sold or built, and any equipment relating to river-craft can be obtained there. The firm is still a family-run business, presently run by Tony Hobbs, a great grandson of the founder. There are always large pleasure launches available for hire, more recently with a Mississippi influence. *Southern Comfort* plied the Thames throughout the seventies and eighties, having taken over from *Pink Champagne.*

Today there is The New Orleans, *largest of all, which has a stern wheel and tall twin smoke stacks, proving very popular indeed for those wishing to celebrate special occasions. Built at Greenwich this elegant vessel cruises between Sonning and Marlow along a beautiful stretch of the Thames Valley, and of course is always part of the Regatta scene.*

LADY HOBBS

MAGIC

WATERMAN TO &H.M THE QUEEN
RIVER TRIPS & BOATS FOR HIRE

HENLEY ON THAMES

Ian Baldwin
1992

24

꧁꧂ MARSH LOCK ꧁꧂

MARSH Lock is the nearest lock to Henley, and one of the most attractive on the River Thames. Modern locks are a fairly recent development, construction starting in the seventeenth century. Previously, to increase the water depth, weirs were built at various places along the river, but unfortunately these hindered navigation and interfered with fishermen and millers. Some weirs, known as flash locks, had moveable sections to allow barges to pass through. Even these caused delays and despite legislative attempts to control them, did not allow the river to fulfil its important role as a highway.

The first modern lock on the Thames was built at Swift Ditch, near Abingdon, in 1630. However it wasn't until the end of the eighteenth century that the locks in the vicinity of Henley were constructed. The person responsible for these was Humphrey Gainsborough, whose brother, Thomas, was the famous artist. Humphrey Gainsborough was the Congregational Minister at Henley who, surprisingly, became very involved with civil engineering. He designed the road which goes up Remenham Hill, worked for the Conways at Park Place, and planned and supervised the construction of locks from Sonning to Hambleden.

Marsh Lock is beautifully situated by a weir between wooded banks, and kept its original flour mill until the Second World War. Now the mill has been converted into flats, and the mill proprietor's house is a private residence. The lock-keeper's cottage is well-kept and adds great charm to the lock itself. Previously operated by hand, to the delight of onlookers waiting to help, the gates now work electrically. This is probably a great relief during Regatta week when the keeper copes with huge volumes of river-traffic. The computerisation of the weirs in the last twenty years has caused the flow of the river to be controlled to a certain extent; Henley now suffers less from flooding.

* * *

Further upstream is Shiplake lock and a favourite spot for holiday homes. Between the two locks the popular local Wargrave and Shiplake regatta is held every August. This is very much a family occasion with a variety of events culminating in the Grand Dongola Race, a greasy pole and a spectacular fireworks display in the evening.

WARNING

Ian Baldwin '92

25

❧❧ FAWLEY COURT ❧❧

FAWLEY Court is a fine mansion to the north of Henley, standing by the river on an ancient site where fallow deer once grazed. Sir James Whitelocke, a nobleman much respected by the people of Henley bought it in 1616. He was reputedly so frightened by the plague of 1625 that he kept all the doors shut, and paid his harvest workers their money by leaving it in a tub of water for collection outside the house.

His son Sir Bulstrode Whitelocke bought the title "Lord of the Manor of Henley" and was very much caught up in the Civil War. Because of his connections with Parliament he was forced to live in his other residence at Phyllis Court nearby. This was garrisoned by Roundheads as Royalist troops were quartered at both Fawley Court and Greenlands while the King was in Oxford. Unfortunately the soldiers plundered Fawley Court, tearing books to pieces to light their tobacco, destroying valuable historical records and killing the deer in the park.

However better times were to come. In 1680 Colonel William Freeman bought the house and commissioned Christopher Wren to create a new residence. Four years later the house was completed and in 1689 visited by William and Mary of Orange. In the eighteenth century the gardens were landscaped by "Capability" Brown, and Sambrooke Freeman asked his designer, James Wyatt, to build the elegant classical temple as a summer-house on the small island opposite the property. The fame of this temple has far exceeded his social aspirations!

In the nineteenth century Fawley Court was sold to the MacKenzie family who restored it even further. During the second World War it was, after so many years, again requisitioned by the army for troops.

In 1953, despite attempts to turn the mansion into a hotel, the Marian Fathers of Poland bought it and founded the Divine College of Mercy there. It offered a haven to Polish boys exiled to camps during the war. The college itself is now closed but retreats are still held there, and many Polish exhibits are on display.

Architecturally the house is rich, with a fine carved ceiling by Grinling Gibbons, Italian paintings and a museum showing a picture of Sarah Freeman whose face was used as a model for "Isis" on Henley's bridge.

The impressive wrought iron gates provide an elegant entrance.

Ian Baldwin 1993

26

GREENLANDS

GREENLANDS can trace its origins back to 1480 when it was part of the ancient estate of Stonor. The original house was nearer to the present Hambleden weir and was known as the Manor of Greenland.

Its present function as the Henley Management College has an interesting connection with Lady Elizabeth Periam who lived at the house over four hundred years ago. A sister of Lord Chancellor Bacon, she was married three times, her first husband being Robert D'Oyley of Norman descent. She is best known for her interests in promoting education, endowing Balliol College with a Fellowship and two scholarships. In 1609 she founded a charity school in Henley and there is an alabaster monument to her in St. Mary's Church.

After her death Greenlands reverted back to the D'Oyley family. In 1643 during the Civil War it was occupied by Royalist troops, but when the Roundheads' counter-attack took place in May 1644, after a six-month siege, the house was in ruins. Sir John D'Oyley then sold the estate to his neighbour Sir Bulstrode Whitelocke. It was bought by Edward Majorbanks in 1853, and considerably enlarged and improved. Some cannon-balls, relics of the Civil War, were found here at this time.

The next owner in 1872 was W. H. Smith, the newspaper magnate, having already become a Member of Parliament in Disraeli's government, serving as first Lord of the Admiralty and Leader of the House of Commons. When he died in 1891 his widow was created Viscountess Hambleden.

Greenlands was their family home and there was much entertaining with plenty of house parties and a large domestic staff to help. In 1939 it was requisitioned for war use; it was the end of an era.

Nowadays it is known as the Henley Management College, has a Royal Charter and is the centre for the training of young executives and for further education in a variety of fields. It holds art exhibitions and Jill Tweed's statue of "The Wrestlers" is on the front lawn.

Lady Elizabeth Periam would surely be delighted to know that her family home of so long ago is now an establishment which fosters her greatest interest – education.

Jan Baldwin 1993

27

HAMBLEDEN MILL

"The rush of the water, and the booming of the mill, bring a dreamy deafness, which seems to heighten the peacefulness of the scene."

(George Eliot).

HAMBLEDEN Mill was first recorded in the Domesday Book. It was one of many ancient mills along the banks of the Thames, built to use water power to drive the wheel for grinding corn and making flour. The ownership of Hambleden Mill passed to the Abbot of Keynsham in 1235; but a second mill was acquired in 1338, disappearing later without a trace.

During the Middle Ages many millers tended to be rogues, frequently allowing themselves more than the customary one tenth of the produce. Those whose livelihoods were in Thameside mills were also at constant warfare with the fishermen and the bargemen, each using the river for a different purpose. By the eighteenth century England possessed twenty thousand watermills, most of them for corn. As recently as 1955, Hambleden Mill, probably rebuilt in the sixteenth century, was still grinding corn and producing flour, using a water-turbine in place of the old water-wheel. Most corn is now milled by steel rollers in factories, although it is still possible to obtain stone-ground flour.

Today the white weatherboarded mill is a landmark, and has been converted into private flats. A footpath crosses the river by the weir, making it accessible for all to see how picturesque this historic building really is.

*   *   *   *   *

Pictured here is the nearby Hambleden Church which is of Norman origin. Situated opposite a pretty village green surrounded by old brick and flint houses, St. Mary's is remarkably unchanged today. St. Thomas de Cantilupe, the last Englishman to be canonised before the Reformation, was baptised in the great stone font by the front door. In the north transept there is a carved alabaster monument to Sir Cope d'Oyley and his wife Martha, with their ten children. In the south transept is an altar which has recently been made from carved oak, said to have been part of Cardinal Wolsey's bedstead, and bearing his arms and hat.

The church tower was added in 1721. Major George Howson, who organised the poppy factory for the British Legion, is buried in the churchyard. The gabled, early seventeenth-century manor house, home of the Hambleden family, completes this scene of an unspoilt Chiltern village set in beautiful surroundings of beechwoods and hills.

Jan Baldwin 1993

28

STONOR PARK

STONOR Park is set in lovely wooded country about five miles from Henley. The estate has passed through the Stonor family almost without exception from father to son for eight hundred years, a remarkable record for this country. Famous for its deer park, its fortunes were in fact founded on wool and successful marriages. The original hall of the twelfth century grew from a small building with a chapel to a grand Tudor mansion. In the sixteenth century it was covered with brick to give the appearance we know so well today.

Because the Stonor family have always been staunch Roman Catholics they were, since the time of the Reformation, deprived of public office and forced to live very privately. The children had to go to France for their education, but the family remained firm in their beliefs. They were brave enough to house the priest Edmund Campion who found a safe refuge in a hidden room to write and publish his book *Decem Rationes* or the *Ten Reasons for Being a Catholic*. Sadly he was later discovered at Wantage, and after transfer to London he was tortured and sent to the gallows. There is an exhibition on his life that can be seen today adjacent to the secret room he used in the gable over the front door.

The family continued to pay heavy fines for their persistent religious beliefs, but after the Emancipation Act of 1829 they could again take part in public affairs. In 1838 Queen Victoria granted Thomas Stonor the ancient Barony of Camoys, inherited from his great-grandmother. He entered into all aspects of life at that time, and was a co-founder of the Henley Royal Regatta. During the 1970s the family suffered financial problems but these were resolved by the present Lord Camoys and now the great house is open to the public.

The approach to Stonor Park is very impressive, along a winding drive up into a pretty valley in the hills.

Fortitude and Temperance

The main entrance has spectacular semicircular steps with carvings on each side of the porch and above, showing Prudence and Justice, Our Lady of Mercy, and Fortitude and Temperance.

Inside the house are many treasures including Italian paintings, family portraits, Flemish tapestries and priceless furniture. The library contains many illegally-printed books used when Stonor was a centre of the Catholic faith. It is a rare achievement that throughout the entire period of religious persecution Mass was celebrated without a break.

29

GREYS COURT

TWO miles to the west of Henley, in the parish of Rotherfield Greys, is the Tudor mansion of Greys Court. Situated in the picturesque hills and beechwoods of South Oxfordshire, the property can trace its origins back to the Domesday Book. In 1239 Walter de Grey, Archbishop of York, acquired it for his brother, Robert, whose grandson John was granted a barony by Edward I.

After the battle of Crecy, Lord de Grey was given a licence by Edward III to crenellate and fortify Greys Court. The house passed to various families over the years, mainly through heiresses, until 1969 when Sir Felix Brunner handed it over to the National Trust.

The original layout of Greys Court consisted of two main quadrangles and two gatehouses. The outline of their foundations can be seen today in dry weather when the grass becomes parched. There are four surviving towers, a keep, stable and well-house. The "Cromwellian Stables" are said to have been used as a messroom by the Roundhead soldiers in the Civil War. It contains a Flemish bridal chest, said to be the one used in the ballad of the "Mistletoe Bough", and large enough to contain many brides! The ancient well is very deep; its huge wheel used to be worked by a donkey.

The house itself has changed over the centuries, the present one being mainly Elizabethan. The drawing room has a ceiling beautifully plastered in the Italian style, and has a fine marble fireplace. The constant occupation by different families for centuries has resulted in a home with many individual features, and some valuable paintings and miniatures. The eighteenth-century staircase and dining-room, together with an updated medieval kitchen, make it a charming residence of a manageable size that today's visitor can appreciate.

The gardens are lovely with many beautiful plants and trees, a ha-ha and an Archbishop's Maze, inspired by an address Dr. Runcie gave in 1981 and based on Christian symbolism.

*   *   *

Less than a mile away is Rotherfield Greys church,

restored in the nineteenth century. It contains a fine brass in the chancel to Sir Robert de Grey, depicted in armour with a lion at his feet. In the Knollys Chapel is a huge monument to this family, who were great supporters of Elizabeth I, with further memorials to the Stapleton family. The church owes its living to Trinity College, Oxford.

Ian Baldwin 1993

30

❧❧ THE BOTTLE AND GLASS ❧❧

THIS charming inn with its thatched roof and ornamental birds has been a popular pub for many years. Early references in 1764 describe it as an ideal stopping place for stage-coaches travelling overland from Henley. This old highway used to turn right at the Plough and pass by the Bottle and Glass at Binfield Heath.

The building itself is very old indeed, with a huge fireplace inside and exposed medieval beams. In 1774 an inn-keeper called William Harris bought the ale-house from a Sonning spinster for the princely sum of £59! In those days the publicans worked very long hours and often found it difficult to make a living, sometimes taking on extra jobs to help pay their way. To obtain a licence the landlord had to find two respectable householders prepared to pay £10 security each to ensure orderly conduct in his pub each year.

From 1779 to 1786 the Appleton brewery acted as one of Harris' sureties for the "Bottle and Glass" and in 1785 and 1786 Robert Brakspear was the other surety. In 1787 Appleton bought the inn from Harris for £110 to clear his debts, and then leased it back to him on condition that he bought his ale and beer from the Appleton Brewery only. This was the start of the tied-house system in the Henley area. As more and more pubs became "tied" to their brewers, prices were forced up. The Bottle and Glass clients experienced an 86% increase in thirteen years! By 1812 Brakspears had amalgamated with Appletons.

In 1822, the Bottle and Glass and the Plough were the only two inns within the Shiplake parish required to pay extra rates for the church's restoration. In 1881 William Brakspear purchased the freeholds of many pubs, including the Bottle and Glass, thereby strengthening his firm's control of the brewery business.

Still one of the traditional Brakspear inns, the Bottle and Glass is no longer on a main highway (which now goes to Reading) but its secluded position makes the trip there very worthwhile; it is a delight to arrive at this picturesque pub at any time of the year. The pleasant choice can be eating out of doors on a summer's day; or feasting at scrubbed wooden farm tables inside by a roaring open fire in winter.

Jan Baldwin '92

31

❧❧ HARPSDEN CHURCH ❧❧

ABOUT a mile to the south of Henley, in a pleasantly secluded valley, is the village of Harpsden. Virtually unchanged since the Domesday Book of 1086, it is in two parts. The manor (or Harpsden Court), the Church and the farm form one group; further up the valley, the village houses and parochial school form the other.

The parish itself is five hundred years old, consisting of both Harpsden and Bolney, the latter including its river frontage. It is a long and relatively narrow parish, being about six miles in length and never more than a mile wide. Set in this peaceful, rural countryside whose landscape, apart from a few new buildings, has little altered in appearance since the reign of Queen Elizabeth I, is the parish church of St. Margaret of Antioch.

The church is built over an underground stream recently discovered near the present font, and probably dates from the twelfth century. It is possible that the early Christians in Harpsden used this small stream for baptisms. A blocked doorway on the south wall and the piscina in the chancel also date from this very early period.

The plan is typically Norman, with a nave separated from the chancel by an arch. Built of local flint and stone, the original windows were small with rounded tops; these were replaced in the fourteenth century by larger ones with Gothic arches. The present chancel replaced the earlier Norman apse at this time as well.

There are several brasses inside the church, including one to Sir Humphrey Forster and his wife in the fifteenth century, and one to Walter Elmes, rector in 1511. In a recess in the south chancel wall is a recumbent stone effigy of a Crusader Knight complete with dog at his feet and (broken) sword.

After the Reformation the rectors were appointed alternately by the Forsters of Harpsden Court and the Elmes of Bolney. In 1639 All Souls' College in Oxford took over the patronage.

By 1803 the church was in need of considerable restoration. Extensive work, financed by the rector Francis Leighton, was started in 1848 with new choir stalls, a new chancel arch and the installation of an organ. Later contributions from the parishioners came in 1852 when the nave was restored and the church was extended to the west. St. Peter's vestry was opened in 1975 by the Queen Mother to provide a church hall and meeting room.

Sir Humphrey Forster

Ian Baldwin '92

32

❧❧ HENLEY GOLF CLUB ❧❧

IN the secluded valley of Harpsden Village, about a mile from the centre of town, is the Henley Golf Club. Its relatively modest clubhouse reflects local history as it developed over the best part of ninety years. It is situated on a course which must be unsurpassed for its natural beauty. Hilly and wooded, with an abundance of additionally planted bushes and trees, it is a slice of Chiltern countryside that is a delight for the nature lover as well as the golfer.

It all started in 1905 with the purchase of land by a syndicate which became registered as Bolney Estates Ltd. A nine-hole course was opened two years later, and the 18-hole course saw its first match on Saturday the 16th of May 1908 with 36 holes played by James Braid, the course designer, and Rowland Jones. With Henley being more famous for its aquatic events, the golfing venture was a challenging diversion to both visitors and residents alike. Mr Archibald Rowsell Brakspear, one of the original members of the golf club, is said to have enjoyed strolling around the links and having a friendly chat with the players in his later years.

The club survived and eventually prospered despite occasional financial problems and two world wars. The engraved trophies give the names of prominent earlier members. In 1910 two golfers scored a hole-in-one and by 1912 the longest hole-in-one ever recorded up to that time was made and held until 1928. Fame was achieved in 1939 with a cartoon of Henley golfers in the Tatler!

Since the last war Henley Golf Club has evolved into a modern, business-like establishment with many improvements made to the bar and furnishings of the clubhouse, and the professional shop and lodgings.

Famous golfers who have played here include the English Ryder Club players of 1940, Dai Rees and Henry Cotton. Today the sponsored Pro-Am tournaments have not only raised money for various charities but also brought more well-known visitors to the club.

The unusual discovery of a Roman Villa of large dimensions was made in 1951 by archeologists excavating near the thirteenth hole. Golfing at Henley can produce its surprises; dogs, ancient ruins and rabbit burrows. A birdie on this course can mean the real thing!

*　　*　　*　　　　　　　　　　　　　　　　　　　　*　　*　　*

Another golf club near Henley is Badgemore Park whose clubhouse has been converted from the stables of the original mansion nearby.

33

❧❧ HARPSDEN BARNS ❧❧

T WO of the most unusual farm buildings in England are situated in Harpsden village. One is a barn and the other a cart shed. They are distinctive in that they are decorated with carved wooden blocks, originally designed for printing calico wallpaper.

The farm itself was part of the Harpsden Court estate for many centuries. The grand old manor house at first consisted of four courts, each facing a point on the compass. In the reign of James I its size had increased to contain seven halls, including a "Beggars' Hall" possibly denoting the distribution of alms from there. At the beginning of the nineteenth century the three remaining sides of one of these courts were pulled down, destroying thirty-four rooms in the process. Unfortunately a Henry VII chimney-piece was also removed! Further alterations took place in 1889 revealing a secret passage dated 1513; sadly, this too was sealed up.

The Forster family lived in Harpsden Court from the fifteenth to the seventeenth century. Famous visitors to this great hall have included Queen Mary in 1553, Queen Elizabeth in 1601 and Oliver Cromwell in 1644.

The old carved, patterned blocks were obtained at Harpsden Court by Lady Grenville last century. As they were no longer required for printing wallpaper, she is thought to have used them to panel a room in a shooting-lodge on the Harpsden estate. When this lodge was demolished after the First World War, Colonel Nobel, who now owned both the Court and the farm, decided to use them to decorate the two barns opposite.

The wood-blocks are carved in various floral patterns in the style of William Morris, although they may be from an even earlier period, perhaps Regency. Their present good condition is due to their hard-wearing wood, thought to have come from central America. They have been fixed onto metal plates and held in position by wooden pins.

The result is extremely eye-catching, and these unique barns now attract the attention of many visitors, most notably that of the late Queen Mary when she visited Harpsden Court.

Jan Baldwin '92

34

🌿🌿 THE PLOWDEN ARMS 🌿🌿

THROUGHOUT its life the Plowden Arms has been a landmark on the road out of Henley at Shiplake. Situated at a prominent bend in the highway it was a welcoming stage-post for traffic travelling overland to Binfield Heath and Goring.

The structure probably dates from the sixteenth century when it consisted of three or four cottages. It has a connection with the Plowden family through the famous Elizabethan lawyer Edmund Plowden, who acquired Shiplake Court in 1573.

Records show that the pub was an ale-house as early as 1749 when an annual fee of £10 was levied on the landlord. However it probably sold beer long before that. By 1775 it was known as The Plough, with Robert Brakspear paying the annual surety, or security, of £10, four years before the Henley Brewery was established.

Brakspear and Sons bought the pub along with several others a few years later. The popular Plough was always chosen for the dinner held after parish meetings, and the signing of The Branch Line Railway Agreement took place there in 1853. The first meeting had been attended by the famous engineer, Brunel, and the extension was funded in part by the citizens of Henley.

For almost a century the Porter family ran The Plough, and were very involved in village activities. Owen Porter rang the bells in the parish church from 1897 to 1908. A celebration bell-ringers' dinner menu can be seen in the bar today, showing a fare of typically English food; possibly the boiled mutton has gone out of fashion!

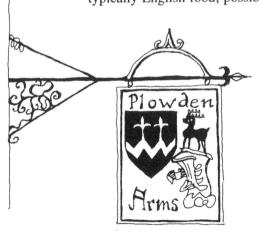

During this period the inn was used for other activities. An undertaker carried out his work from here, keeping his "clients'" bodies in the cellar alongside the beer, while he made their coffins! Another pub story is about the foreman's bowler hat which was thrown as a joke by his workmen down a 90 ft well near the main entrance. (This is fortunately sealed off today). In order not to lose face, the foreman was lowered down the well on a rope, to retrieve his precious status symbol!

*   *   *

In 1936 after the name had been changed to The Plowden Arms, a new pub-sign, designed by Major Sheppard, was entered at the Inn Sign Exhibition in London. It came tenth out of 280 exhibits, and it includes the correct arms of the Plowden family, awarded by King Richard I to Roger de Plowden in 1194.

❧❧ SHIPLAKE COLLEGE ❧❧

JUST over two miles upstream of Henley, set in beautiful surroundings next to the parish church and overlooking a spectacular bend of the river, is Shiplake College. Founded in 1959 it is one of England's most recent public schools, yet enjoys an ancient historical background through its main building, Shiplake Court. Although this present mansion with its red and grey patterned bricks was constructed in 1890, the estate includes a much earlier tithe barn and a Tudor cottage.

Shiplake Court has been occupied for seven hundred years. By the fourteenth century it belonged to the Englefield family who supported the Roman Catholic cause at the time of the Reformation. Queen Elizabeth confiscated all lands belonging to Sir Francis Englefield and these were subsequently leased by the crown in 1573 to Sir Edmund Plowden and his family, also Catholics, from Shropshire. This family's connection ended in 1688 with the downfall of James II.

The following year the Jennings family acquired the property. It fell into decay in the eighteenth century and was sold in 1802 for demolition. The grounds were now known as Shiplake Court Farm.

In 1888 Mr Robert Harrison, a city stockbroker, bought the property and built the Tudor-style mansion, setting out the grounds and main buildings very much as they are today. His wife furnished the house lavishly, and the gardens were often used for local events. Sadly, their elder son Cecil was killed in the First World War, and their grandson Ralph died in the Royal Air Force in World War Two.

The BBC bought Shiplake Court for £15,000 in 1941, putting it up for sale in 1958. Mr and Mrs Alec Everett then acquired it for educational purposes and the College was officially opened on 1st May 1959. Its aim was to attract less academic boys requiring a modified curriculum.

The College has gone from strength to strength over the years. Its relatively small size and small classes are both great assets. Music and the arts prosper, and sport plays an important part in school life. There are five houses for the boys,

a large sports hall and an impressive new classroom block. Drama is popular; a most ambitious performance in 1979, *Time and the Thames,* took place on the river, and was a pageant of English history based on the river in which original Dunkirk boats took part.

✳   ✳   ✳

The unusual Victorian water-tower within the grounds completes this modern public school.

SHIPLAKE CHURCH

"Vicar of this pleasant spot
Where it was my chance to marry
Happy, happy be your lot
In the vicarage by the quarry.
You were he that knit the knot."

THESE lines by Alfred Lord Tennyson were written on the morning of his wedding in 1850 to Emily Selwood. She was a cousin of the wife of the vicar of Shiplake Church and the marriage took place from the old vicarage nearby.

The ancient church of St. Peter and St. Paul stands high on a hill overlooking the Thames. It is indeed a "pleasant spot". The view of the river is breathtaking and must have inspired many less famous poets with its beauty. The church has been there since the twelfth century, the oldest parts being the Lady Chapel, and the tower which was separate at first. They were joined together by the nave a century later. Considerable restoration has been carried out since then, particularly in the nineteenth century.

Items of interest include the twelfth-century piscina to the right of the altar in the Lady Chapel, and one thirteenth-century stone pillar in the nave. There is a fifteenth-century canopied chair, probably French, in the sanctuary, an Elizabethan chalice, communion plate and monumental brasses. The pulpit installed in 1980 is of Jacobean Oak. Perhaps the most significant feature of the church is the medieval stained glass from the ruined abbey of St. Bertin in St. Omer. This was removed during the French revolution. It was presented to the vicar of Shiplake in 1828 by his friend the Rev. J. P. Boteler, and carefully restored to make the four lovely windows that can be seen today.

There are eight bells which ring out over the village for services. When Tennyson was married there were five, and in the reign of Edward VI only three. The Lady Chapel altar is a memorial to the men of Shiplake who fell in the First World War. Every Remembrance Sunday a service is held in honour of all who lost their lives in two world wars, and wreaths are laid at the War Memorial in Shiplake.

*   *   *

Lashbrook Chapel is a delightful small weatherboard building which may have been a paper store for Shiplake Mill. Services have been held there regularly since the mill was pulled down in 1907.

SOME IMPORTANT DATES IN HENLEY

World Events in italics

1204   King John gave the patronage of St. Mary's Church to Americus de Harcourt

1400   The Chantry House was built

1473   John Longland, later Bishop of Lincoln, born in Henley

1531   The Red Lion Hotel was built

1540   The Church Tower of St. Mary's was built

1588   *Spanish Armada defeated*

1601   Queen Elizabeth slept at Harpsden Court

1604   King James I founded Henley Grammar School

1609   Lady Periam's School founded

1616   Sir James Whitelock bought Fawley Court

1616   *Shakespeare died*

1630   First modern lock 'Swift Ditch' built on the Thames near Abingdon

1642   Prince Rupert hanged a Parliamentary spy on an elm tree in Henley

1643   Phyllis Court fortified by Roundheads

1649   *Charles I executed*

1666   *Great Fire of London*

1680   Christopher Wren created a new residence at Fawley Court

1710   *St. Paul's Cathedral completed*

1770   *Captain Cook discovered Australia*

1771   James Wyatt commissioned to build 'Temple Island'

1773   Most locks from Marlow to Sonning completed

1774   The 'Bottle and Glass' bought for £59 from a Sonning spinster

1774   Old wooden bridge swept away in a storm

1776   *American War of Independence took place*

1779   Robert Brakspear came to Henley

1786   The new Henley Bridge was built

1789   *The French Revolution occurred*

1790   The middle row of houses in Hart Street was demolished

1795   The Old Town Hall replaced the Guildhall

1805   The Kenton Theatre held its first performance

1815   *The Battle of Waterloo took place*

1818	The Leander Club was founded
1829	The first Oxford/Cambridge boat-race was held from Hambleden to Henley
1837	*Queen Victoria came to the throne*
1839	The first Henley Regatta was held
1850	Tennyson was married in Shiplake Church
1851	*The Great Exhibition was held in London*
1857	The Twyford-Henley branch of the railway line opened
1872	W. H. Smith bought Greenlands
1873	The first American crews rowed at the Regatta
1891	W. H. Smith's widow became Viscountess Hambleden
1901	*Queen Victoria died*
1901	New Henley Town Hall completed
1905	Henley Golf Club founded
1906	Phyllis Court becomes a club
1908	First Rowing Olympics at Henley
1914	*Outbreak of First World War*
1919	The Stewards Enclosure was opened
1931	*Empire State building opened*
1939	*Outbreak of Second World War*
1941	Discovery of a Roman Villa in Harpsden
1948	Second Rowing Olympics were held at Henley
1959	Shiplake College founded
1969	Greys Court passed to National Trust
1974	Market Place renamed Falaise Square
1986	Regatta Headquarters opened by the Queen
1987	The Henley College opened; first Tertiary College in Oxfordshire
1993	Award-winning Grandstand Pavilion at Phyllis Court built
1994	*The Channel Tunnel officially opened*

FURTHER READING

The Story of Henley, Geoffrey Hollingworth (1983)

Henley-on-Thames – a Pictorial History, Ann Cottingham and Hilary Fisher (1990)

The Book of Henley-on-Thames, G. H. J. Tomalin (1975)

Views of Henley-on-Thames, Margaret Shaida (1984)

The Henley-on-Thames Branch, Paul Karan (1982)

Henley Royal Regatta – 1839-1989, Souvenir Magazine

A Guide to Henley-on-Thames (1896), Emily Climenson

A History of Shiplake, Emily Climenson

Brakspear's Brewery – 1779-1979, Francis Sheppard (1979)

Wish and Fulfilment, H. E. Wells-Furby (1984)

The Phyllis Court Story, Angela Perkins (1983)

The Chilterns and the Thames Valley, Paul Felix (1992)

Around Henley-on-Thames in Old Photographs, Siân Ellis (1992)

Henley Golf Club – the First 80 Years, Laureen Williamson (1986)

Henley-on-Thames and its Vicinity, printed and published by E. Kinch, Market Place, 1866

Guide to Stonor Park – published by Stonor Enterprises

Guide to Greys Court – National Trust (1986)

and various other brochures relating to specific buildings and churches, etc.

Historic Churches of the Thames Valley, Graham Martin (1973)

Nicholson's *Guide to the Thames – from Source to Sea*

Salters *Guide to the Thames*

Henley Town Badge